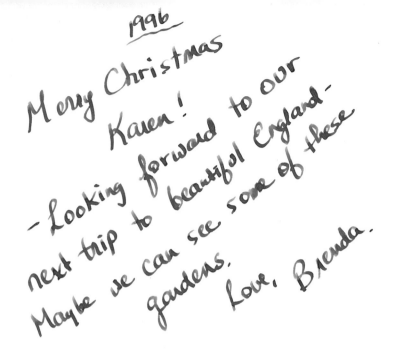

1996

Merry Christmas
Karen!
- Looking forward to our
next trip to beautiful England -
Maybe we can see some of these
gardens.
Love, Brenda.

THE ENGLISH COTTAGE GARDEN

The English Cottage Garden

Jane Taylor and Andrew Lawson

Weidenfeld and Nicolson
London

Half-title page illustration

Collingbourne Ducis, Wiltshire

A cosy thatched roof, a whitewashed wall on which the sun throws the shadows of stately pink hollyhocks: all that is best about the English cottage and its garden is in this simple vignette.

Frontispiece

Hook Norton, Oxfordshire

Roses on the wall, foxgloves at their feet, a 'gothic' window, a wooden fence for a stone-built cottage: simple components, adding up to a picture that could be the result of happy accident or studied planning.

Text © Jane Taylor 1994
Photographs © Andrew Lawson 1994

First published in Great Britain in 1994 by
George Weidenfeld & Nicolson Limited
The Orion Publishing Group
Orion House, 5 Upper St Martin's Lane
London WC2H 9EA

British Library Cataloguing in Publication Data
A catalogue for this book is available from the British Library

Designed by Ronald Clark

Printed and bound in Italy

Contents

Owslebury, Hampshire

The idealized cottage garden of the twentieth century draws on the traditions of earlier centuries, with a generous helping of nostalgia for the past. Surrounding this cottage, with its thatched roof and its roses, is a garden of this kind. The planting is characteristically profuse, with a range of plants that includes the old-fashioned and the modern. Some of the plants we now regard as typically old-fashioned cottage-garden plants are themselves not natives, but imports. The first exotics to reach England came from southern Europe, such as wallflowers and clove pinks and the old double red cottage peony (*Paeonia officinalis* 'Rubra Plena'), and from the east, among them the oriental poppy (*Papaver orientale*). As more and more exotic plants found their way into the gardens and hothouses of the gentry, slips and roots of the older plants, which were hardy enough to survive outside, must often have passed from the gardeners 'up at the big house' into the hands of their cottager neighbours, to grow alongside the native plants cherished for their utility or curiosity.

Cottages and Cottage Gardens of the Past

Streatley, Berkshire

The irregular, knobbly contours of flint do not lend themselves to straight lines and sharp angles, so the surrounds of doors and windows are made of brick, the warm terracotta contrasting with the steely grey and chalk-white of the split flints. This cottage is in a region with ready access to a diversity of building materials, so the path in front of the cottage is made of paving slabs and gravel, walls and path together giving a tapestry of textures to set off the profusion of late summer flowers.

For such a small country, England's landscapes are very diverse, and her cottages no less varied. The south has its rolling chalk downs, its narrow and secretive lanes plunging through ancient mixed woodlands, its noble beechwoods; to the north of the great River Thames that runs through London lie the flat lands and huge skies of Essex and East Anglia, names that go back to the days of invasions from continental Europe. Here, the cottages are generally half-timbered, with brick or wattle and daub, entirely brick-built with slate roofs, or wholly of timber, with clapboard walls. In chalk and clay country they would often be built of cob (trodden clay mixed with straw), with a thatched roof. Where stone dominates, as in the hilly limestone spine that runs from Dorset in the south to Yorkshire in the north, or on the granite moors of Cornwall or the bleak hills of the Lake District in the north-west, the cottages are more likely to be stone-built. In flint country the flint walls are often held together with lacing courses of brickwork. Whatever the choice

Great Tew, Oxfordshire, and Sankyns Green, Hereford and Worcester

The diversity of England's cottages makes it hard to name a 'typical' cottage style. Nonetheless, many people have in their minds two images that seem to epitomize the cottages of England: half-timbered, whitewashed, with tiled or thatched roof, and the stone-built cottages of the limestone backbone of England. Even rimed with winter frost, the stone cottages of Great Tew (*left*) in Oxfordshire look cosy and welcoming, while in early summer this half-timbered Worcestershire cottage (*right*) is embowered in a profusion of flowers.

Whiddon Down, Devon

Cottages in exposed regions, by the coast or high on the moors were generally low-built, huddling down against the force of the gales sweeping off the Atlantic. The plants in their gardens have to be tough, too, though in the lee of the cottage there is shelter for some choicer flowers. The orange montbretia at the foot of the boundary wall is an indestructible non-native.

Clifton Hampden, Oxfordshire

Away from the regions where building stone was so abundant that it was the obvious choice for mansion, church and cottage alike, different materials might be used side by side in the same village; here a half-timbered cottage with brick infill, sharing a wall with another built entirely of brick, with tiled roof, stands next to a thatched cottage built of whitewashed cob on stone foundations.

there is always a kind of rightness about cottages built with local materials. They have a timeless look about them, a sense of unself-conscious ease, that the grander mansions often lack.

As well as the cottages built by and for the yeoman farmers and landless workers of England, since the end of the eighteenth century, under the influence of the movement known as the Picturesque, cottages for the well-to-do have been a feature of the English landscape. Architect-designed and self-consciously in the vernacular style, some of these are almost as big as mansions; but their style looks back to the simplicity of the genuine cottage rather than to classical architecture. Whereas the peasant's cottage was often rudely built, without even the basic amenities of the day, and hopelessly cramped – perhaps of only one or two rooms – the Picturesque cottage was designed to enable the gentry to enjoy the simple life in comfort. The earliest of these architect-designed cottages were in the style known as rustic, the wide overhang of their thatched roofs supported by rough posts up which creepers – honeysuckle, jasmine or ivy – could be trained. Another enduringly popular style was known as Old English; such cottages, often built of stone or half-timbered brick, harked back to the gothic architecture of the Middle Ages, and the gardens that surrounded them were frequently designed to recall Tudor formal gardens, right down to the selection of plants.

Much of what we know of the earliest cottage gardens has reached us indirectly, through the works of writers such as Chaucer and Langland. Chaucer's *Canterbury Tales*, a collection of narratives recounted by a group of pilgrims making their way to Canterbury, date from 1386 or 1387. A line here, a short passage there in the Prologue, and in the tales Chaucer attributes to his characters, create a picture of the cottages of husbandmen and small farmers, surrounded by a yard mainly given over to livestock, but with a patch for vegetables and herbs. From William Langland's *Piers Plowman* of *c.*1385 we learn that the poor lived almost wholly on fruit and vegetables, with the occasional rabbit poached from manorial lands: 'Beans and baked apples . . . cibolles [scallion or Welsh onion] and . . . ripe cherries'.

Chaucer mentioned very few plants by name, but we learn more of the plants likely to be grown in gardens from a treatise in verse, *The Feaste of Gardening*, written by Jon the Gardener soon after Chaucer's death in 1400. He lists chiefly native plants, valued no doubt for their medicinal qualities or as strewing herbs as well as for the pot. Among the introduced plants he recommends are southernwood or lad's love (*Artemisia abrotanum*), hyssop, rue or herb of grace and sage – all from southern Europe, and all strongly aromatic – and the Madonna lily, *Lilium candidum*, a native of the eastern Mediterranean.

How did the cottage garden progress from the yard with more livestock than vegetables of Chaucer's day to today's idealized picture? The likelihood is that for centuries, even in times of prosperity, many of those who formed the labouring class lived in hovels scarcely worthy to be called cottages; only the more sturdily built dwellings have survived, and they would have belonged to yeoman farmers and country craftsmen or artisans such as the village blacksmith, rather than to the labourers. And even they would have seen

Madonna Lily

The Madonna lily grown in English gardens was already of great antiquity when Jon the Gardener included it in his list in the early fifteenth century; it was introduced by the Romans, and had then probably already been in cultivation for a thousand years or more. An older name for it is cottage lily; a very apt one, for to this day it seems to grow better in cottage gardens, left undisturbed year after year, than in grander domains. It was valued not only for its beauty but also for its medicinal qualities: it was said to cure boils, corns, dropsy and even wrinkles. Its variants with double flowers, with purple-spotted flowers, and with yellow-edged leaves, are lost to cultivation, but the old plant of the Romans is still with us.

Clove Pinks

For centuries the most common beverage of the English labourer was ale. This cloudy brew, which was doubtless safer than the water to drink, might be flavoured with clove-scented pinks, the ancestor of which (*Dianthus caryophyllus*) was brought over at the time of the Norman Conquest, perhaps accidently along with the Caen stone imported to build abbeys. Used also to flavour wine, these old, strongly fragrant pinks – an older name is clove gilloflower – were known as sops in wine; in Chaucer's day they grew in every alehouse garden. In Chaucer's own words:

> *And many a clove gilofre*
> *And nutmeg to put in ale*
> *Whether it be moist or stale.*

Some say the clove gilofre was the spice, not the flower: the French for cloves is *clous de girofle*, so there is some similarity in the name. But spices were costly in those days, and clove-scented pinks would have been a far cheaper, home-grown substitute.

their garden plots as largely utilitarian, a place to grow vegetables and herbs, to keep bees for honey and chickens for the pot.

In the main, the affairs of the peasantry were of little concern to the literate classes until comparatively recent times. However, Shakespeare's characters, two centuries after Chaucer and Langland, include peasants as well as nobles and kings; and in the bard's plays many flowers are mentioned. Shakespeare himself did not belong to the gentry, let alone the nobility: he was the son of a merchant who dealt in corn, hides and wood. His wife Anne Hathaway's cottage, with its flowery garden, can be seen to this day in Shottery, near Stratford-upon-Avon, Shakespeare's birthplace.

Gerard was a contemporary of Shakespeare's who wrote specifically about plants; his famous *Herball* of 1597 includes the earliest evidence that many of our familiar cottage garden flowers were already in cultivation in England. Drawing on the knowledge of ancient physicians, he wrote of the medicinal qualities and other useful attributes of the plants – the very qualities that would have been of most interest to the cottagers, though few of them would have been able to read the *Herball*, still less afford to purchase a copy.

More helpful to us as a guide to the Elizabethan cottage garden is a book of verse dating from 1557 by Thomas Tusser, called *A Hundred Good Points of Husbandry* and addressed to tenant farmers and their wives. From Tusser we learn that the small farmer had a garden, which his wife was expected to care for, and an orchard. He lists a great many plants, most of them grown for the table – vegetables, and herbs to flavour them, salads (to judge from the

Shottery, Warwickshire

Anne Hathaway's cottage, half-timbered and thatched, is seen here through one of the most characteristic of cottage garden flowers, the hollyhock. This was one of the plants Thomas Tusser recommended for ornament in the farmer's wife's garden; from Gerard we learn that in the sixteenth century it was already available in white, red and deep purple, and that a double purple was known as well.

Bledlow, Buckinghamshire

This substantial black-and-white cottage may well have belonged to a yeoman farmer, making a prosperous living from the fertile land at the foot of the chalky Chiltern Hills, while his wife tended the garden as described by Thomas Tusser, filling it with herbs and vegetables and flowers to make into fragrant waters.

diversity of salad plants, the English must have been much better at salad-making in the sixteenth century than for most of the twentieth), flowers and fruits for preserving and stilling, a score of herbs for strewing on the floor against lice, fleas and bad smells, and others for medicinal use. As well as these utilitarian plants – of which some at least, such as roses for stilling, would have been beautiful as well – Tusser lists flowers that the farmer's wife could grow in pots, or pick to bring indoors, purely for their decorative value. But he has nothing to say about how they might be arranged in the garden.

Between 1570 and the Revolution of 1640 many of England's villages were transformed, thereafter to remain substantially unchanged until the mid-twentieth century. The village school and inn, the almshouses, and many of the better cottages were built then. Another wave of building took place from quite early in the eighteenth century, lasting until into the early nineteenth: the model villages, built by landlords for their labourers, at first for aesthetic reasons, to replace the eyesore of ramshackle hovels or as part of the creation of an ideal landscape, and later from philanthropic motives. The less conscientious landlords, it must be said, were known to pull down the hovels and leave the cottagers to fend for themselves, landless and homeless, often with their commoners' rights forfeited as well, as the landowner enclosed open land for his own use. The more fortunate found themselves with productive gardens, where they could rear livestock and grow vegetables and flowers.

At much the same time as landlords were building model villages,

**Little Brington,
Northamptonshire**

The fashion for growing plants
in pots, whether crowding the
cottage windowsills or stood in
odd corners outside, endures to
this day. A tub of pansies
brings a touch of vivid colour
to the sombre stone.

**Sankyns Green,
Hereford and Worcester**

Among the oldest of cultivated roses is the apothecary's rose, *Rosa gallica officinalis*. It flowers only once, in summer, but its fragrance is irresistible and it is thrifty and hardy. The industry of making confections and conserves from its petals developed as long ago as the thirteenth century, in the French town of Provins; the rose grew there in great quantity, and the industry lasted for more than six centuries. It was certainly an early introduction to England: it was the emblem chosen by the House of Lancaster (whose rivals, the House of York,

chose the white rose, *Rosa alba*) in the struggle for the throne of England which became known as the Wars of the Roses and which ended with the victory of King Henry VII, first of the Tudor kings, in 1485. The striped sport of the apothecary's rose, properly known as *Rosa gallica* 'Versicolor', is also known as 'Rosa Mundi' and popularly associated with the Fair Rosamond of King Henry II, who died in 1176; a historian of roses speculates that 'perhaps an earlier Crusader found the striped form in a Syrian garden, and on his return presented it to her after giving it her name'.

there began the fashion for the gentry to live in houses of cottage style, achieving a lifestyle of studied simplicity with the help of indoor and outdoor staff. The cottage garden as we know it today derives from these two strands, the subsistence and the romantic, at first distinct but later merging until it is hardly possible to distinguish between the garden plots of small farmers and artisans, or of labourers fortunate enough to have an enlightened landlord, and the more self-consciously planted gardens around the Picturesque cottages of the gentry.

Nostalgia for a golden past, often thought to belong to the highly industrialized twentieth century, is no new phenomenon. By Victorian times the yearning for an idyllic, innocent rustic past was already well developed. It found expression not only in the building of Picturesque cottages but also in the watercolour paintings of a number of Victorian artists, which show us, as the writers of the day seldom did, what cottage gardens actually looked like. Myles Birket Foster, one of the most famous, painted many cottages, with gardens in which chubby children play; his interest was more in the children than the gardens, however. One artist above all, Helen Allingham, painted cottage gardens for their own sake. Her aim was to record, scrupulously and sympathetically, the old cottages and their gardens before they disappeared for ever. What her paintings show us are profusely planted, flowery, pretty plots.

Two of the late nineteenth- and early twentieth-century gardening writers who have most inspired the twentieth-century English garden are Gertrude Jekyll and William Robinson. Both thought highly of the cottage gardens of their day, and often drew inspira-

Great Tew, Oxfordshire

The village of Great Tew was remodelled in the nineteenth century by John Claudius Loudon, a remarkable man who wrote the massive *Encyclopaedia of Cottage, Farm and Villa Architecture* (1833) as well as a great many books on gardening – books for the owners of the new villas, books for the landed gentry, books for, or at least about, the cottagers. He was in large part responsible for spurring on the philanthropic movement among landowners which led to the improvement of so many cottages, and with it the lot of their tenants.

Helmingham, Suffolk

Model cottages of the nineteenth century are surrounded,
in the late twentieth, by
gardens of impeccable neatness,
such as any landowner would
have applauded in his tenants.
In those days, the head gardener from 'the big house' could
be a great help to the cottagers
by providing them with seeds
and cuttings for their little
plots, and perhaps with advice
and instruction as well.

tion from them. Miss Jekyll wrote 'I have learned much from the little cottage gardens that help to make our English waysides the prettiest in the temperate world', and Robinson claimed that 'English cottage gardens are never bare and seldom ugly . . . among the things made by man nothing is prettier than an English cottage garden, and they often teach lessons that the "great" gardeners should learn.'

The greatest English gardens of the twentieth century, like the architects of the Picturesque before them, have drawn on the humbler traditions of the cottage garden. Two of the most famous, Sissinghurst, in Kent (the south-eastern county which itself is often called 'the garden of England'), and Hidcote Bartrim in the Cotswolds, are what they are because of the generations of unsung cottage gardeners that inspired their creators.

Through the Gate
and Up
the Garden Path

In the Middle Ages the familiar English landscape of fields surrounded by hedges or stone walls was virtually unknown; and even after the open, strip-farmed fields had all been enclosed, by the time Queen Victoria came to the throne in 1837, there remained extensive areas of common land where peasants could pasture their beasts. Cottage gardens, therefore, would always have been surrounded by a wall or hedge or fence, to keep the cottager's produce safe. A simple wooden or wrought-iron gate opened onto a narrow, straight path running at a right-angle from the road or the common to the cottage door. Like the cottage itself, the garden path would be surfaced with local materials – brick, stone, or even simply beaten earth.

Whatever grew near the door would thrive on a diet of dish-water; there was no piped drainage in the cottages of old, so the only way to dispose of slops was out of the door. Beside the path, always to hand, is the ideal place to grow medicinal herbs that were in regular use, or to tuck in the odd treasure – a double-flowered primrose, perhaps, or a violet of special colouring, not the familiar blue or white but pink, sulphur or red – discovered in the fields and hedgerows and brought home as a curiosity. Today, a straight path might be edged with double daisies in pink, red and white (once popular in eighteenth-century London's window boxes, these are now cottage garden plants *par excellence*), or with London pride (*Saxifraga umbrosa* and *S.* × *urbium*) or sea thrift (*Armeria maritima*).

Parham, Suffolk

Even today there remains some unfenced common land, where – at least in theory – cottagers can graze their livestock. The village green today, however, is more likely to host local cricket matches than geese or sheep or cattle. The gardens of these cottages, nonetheless, remain secure behind their fences and gates, echoed by the neat, white-painted porches.

East Coker, Somerset

In the mining and textile villages of the north, it was usual for the rows of terraced cottages to give straight onto the street; the miners had allotments, not gardens, to grow their vegetables and flowers. But elsewhere there was almost always a front garden, no matter how tiny, as in this village where the stone cottages with their thatched roofs have little walled front gardens and trim white gates. Flowers have spilled out even onto the grassy verge that separates the garden gate from the road.

Itteringham, Norfolk

The very first plant to greet the visitor to this cottage is feverfew, with its clusters of brilliant white daisies and finely cut leaves. It is easy to grow, and ready to seed itself about so that once in the garden it will always remain. Gerard describes feverfew or featherfew (from febrifuge, banishing fever) as 'of a strong smell, and bitter taste', which anyone who has chewed the leaves as a remedy for migraine will recognize instantly. Gerard recommended adding honey or sweet wine, perhaps to make it slightly less unpalatable.

Rolvenden, Kent

A simple clapboarded Kent cottage stands at the end of a brick path edged with mossy saxifrage, over which a pink cherry has scattered its fallen petals. Pink-flowered cherries reached England from Japan; the native wild cherry or gean, celebrated by the poet A. E. Housman in *A Shropshire Lad* as 'loveliest of trees', is far too big for a cottage garden, and belongs in the woodlands where Housman went to see it 'wearing white for Eastertide'.

East Coker, Somerset

One of the plants Thomas Tusser recommended to the Tudor farmer's wife for ornament was the hollyhock, to this day a cottage favourite. The glowing red of these hollyhocks is echoed by the scarlet roses on the cottage wall on the other side of the road. The rowan (*Sorbus aucuparia*) to the right, its berries just starting to colour, is a native tree long associated with magic; and magic itself was, in earlier centuries, inextricably bound up with the qualities of plants that gave them the power to heal – or to kill. Rowan is a tree that affords protection to those who grow it. Its berries are bright red; there is no better colour than red against evil. Did those who planted the red hollyhocks and red roses know that, or was the need for red buried deep in their subconscious?

VERANDAH
COTTAGE

East Coker, Somerset

Looking back at the cottage with the rowan tree, we see that another English native plant with magical powers also grows here: ivy. Nowadays it is more often associated in our minds with Christmas, because of the Christmas carol that begins 'The holly and the ivy'; but its link to the festival of midwinter goes back to pre-Christian times. Very few native English plants are evergreen; that ivy not only remains green in winter, but even flowers in autumn to ripen its fruits during the dead of year, gave it a special significance in the days when nature was far more threatening and mysterious than now. To have two such potent plants as ivy and rowan flanking the gate would confer security upon the occupant of the cottage, guarding them against the evil spirits that roamed the world outside the garden walls.

Hidcote Bartrim, Gloucestershire

Every cottage would have had a resident cat, in the old days; not a pampered pedigree animal, but a working cat, whose job was to catch the mice and rats that could easily ruin the stored apples, grain and root vegetables on which the family depended for their winter meals. This marmalade cat, surveying his domain from the vantage point of the gatepost, belongs to that honourable strain of working animals whose partnership with the cottagers was so important.

Helmingham, Suffolk

This cottage garden vignette is composed of the simplest of elements – a white wooden gate, clipped hedges flanking a plain concrete path, a white front door – all heightened by the play of light and shadow. Here too, ivy grows beside the gate.

Ampney Crucis, Gloucestershire

Writing from direct experience of cottage life in the 1880s, Flora Thompson, in her trilogy *Lark Rise to Candleford*, describes 'narrow paths between high, built-up banks supporting flower borders, crowded with jonquils, auriculas, forget-me-nots and other spring flowers' leading from one part of the garden to another. The garden she was describing belonged to someone able to afford an old man from the village one day a week to tend the vegetables; but 'the flower garden was no one's special business . . . the flowers just grew as they would in crowded masses, perfect in their imperfection.' Close planting of this kind, with not an inch of soil to be seen, is typical of the cottage style. Again, the cottage itself is linked to the world beyond the garden by a simple narrow path, of stone this time, the strong simple lines of cottage and path softened by the colourful spring flowers. As the forget-me-nots fade, they can be pulled out in handfuls, leaving space for a summer planting of equal profusion.

Ilmington, Warwickshire

The entrance to this cottage garden recalls the lych gates of country churchyards. The red valerian (*Centranthus ruber*) growing in the wall is a southern European native, introduced during the sixteenth century. It took a while to naturalize itself widely; by 1778, William Hudson was able to record (in his *Flora Anglica*) that it grew on old tumbledown walls in Devon and Cornwall, but even a hundred years later it was said to be rare on Oxford's ancient walls. Today it is everywhere, as much at home on grandiose ruins as in cottage garden walls. In the early days of the 'rustic' cottage, the creeper covering the roof would probably have been ivy; today, with the much wider choice available to gardeners, this free-flowering clematis makes a change from the more conventionally cottagey rose or honeysuckle.

Alfriston, Sussex

The bluebells lit by the spring sunshine are not the English bluebell of oak woodlands, *Hyacinthoïdes non-scripta*, but the fuller-flowered Spanish bluebell, less apt to take over the whole garden with its free-seeding ways. The wild bluebell, unlike so many native plants, seems never to have been a cottage garden plant; it took the poets, above all Keats and Gerard Manley Hopkins in the nineteenth century, to extol its beauty.

Great Tew, Oxfordshire

Clipped hedges swell over the white gate that opens onto the traditional straight path leading to the cottage door, surfaced, as you would expect in this limestone region of stone-built cottages, with flagstones. Almost as handsome as the scarlet tulips and blue grape hyacinths is the rich mahogany young foliage of bush roses, immaculately pruned to ensure plenty of summer blooms after the spring bulbs have gone to ground.

Great Tew, Oxfordshire

Not all the cottage gardens at Great Tew divulge themselves to the casual visitor so readily. Here, mature box hedges have spread sideways until they almost meet over the little wooden gate and the path is almost too narrow to pass. The eye is tantalized by the sense of secretiveness, the shadows that lie just beyond the sun-warmed gate.

Sibford Ferris, Oxfordshire

Crazy paving, where irregular slabs of stone are used to surface a path, has become a cliché, all too often faked in suburban gardens; but it also has an honourable history in cottage gardens where regular flagstones would have been simply too expensive to use. In this garden a narrow paved path leads between flowery borders beneath an apple tree, flanked by a drystone wall built in the traditional Cotswold manner with vertical capping stones. Many of the flowers are natives or happily naturalized in England: Welsh poppies in yellow and the less common orange, the mourning widow or dusky cranesbill (*Geranium phaeum*), named for its sombre slate-purple flowers, columbines in deep plum-pink to tone with the geranium and forget-me-nots.

Itteringham, Norfolk

Bricks laid herringbone-style echo the brick walls of this cottage. The plants in the wall border are predominantly aromatic: thyme, golden marjoram, and a big bush of rosemary. For Thomas Tusser, marjoram was a strewing herb, not one for the kitchen; but both rosemary and marjoram were valued for their flavour, and rosemary flowers, distilled, are recommended by Gerard for taking away 'the stench of the mouth and breath . . . if there be added thereto, to steep or infuse . . . a few Cloves, Mace, Cinnamon, and a little Anise seed'.

Double Primrose

The primrose is one of England's best loved wild flowers, long cultivated as much for its medicinal qualities as its endearing charm. It was used as a dressing for wounds and as an emetic, and was said to cure headaches and to remedy pains in the joints – and there must have been many of those, in the damp, cold cottages of the days before central heating. Surely, though, the aberrant or double forms that sometimes spontaneously occur in the wild must have been cherished simply for their beauty. They are harder to keep than the single-flowered wildling, which regularly renews itself by seed. They must be regularly divided, and need a rich, well-nourished soil that does not dry out, out of the sun, though garden writers of earlier centuries suggest that even the doubles were not then so pernickety as they are now. The earliest reference to a double primrose is in Gerard's *Herball* of 1597, where he describes a double white; the double lilac primrose often called 'Quaker's Bonnet' is almost as ancient.

Cottage Garden Topiary

Topiary – the art of clipping trees and shrubs into formal, elaborate or merely tidy shapes – has ancient roots. We know that the Romans practised it in their villa gardens. Later, in the first great development of the grand English garden style, in the sixteenth century, it was an important element. But it lends itself equally well to humbler surroundings, and when the enthusiasm for Capability Brown's spare, classical landscapes seized the landowning classes of Britain, in the eighteenth century, the art of topiary was kept alive to a great extent by cottagers, for whom such fashionable movements had no relevance. Robert Southey, lesser-known associate of the romantic poets Wordsworth and Coleridge, described a yeoman's garden in the West Riding of Yorkshire which 'you entered between two yew trees clipt to the fashion of two pawns'. Like the cottage itself, topiary was 'rediscovered' and reclaimed by the proponents of the Picturesque, and was also championed by the Arts and Crafts Movement of the late nineteenth century.

The cottager who had become prosperous enough to have time in his garden plot for more than vegetables could clip an imaginary cockyolly bird, or give his hedge a castellated outline in imitation of a castle wall. The most popular medium for topiary was box (*Buxus sempervirens*), a native, or at least naturalized, shrub or small tree found in southern England: Box Hill in the county of Surrey and Boxley in Kent are both named for their box trees. By the late seventeenth century another British native, yew (*Taxus baccata*) had become the favourite for topiary work. Yew had magical properties and was frequently planted by the entrance to a cottage, or near the chimney stack, to protect the house and its occupants from evil spirits. Some were allowed to grow freely to maturity, when they would also shelter the cottage from the prevailing wind; but others must have been clipped from the start, if only for lack of space. Holly and privet – the latter rather coarse, and leafless in winter, but extremely easy and cheap to increase – were also used for hedging and for topiary work.

Sapperton, Gloucestershire

Gloucestershire is the English county that is richest in topiary, thanks in large part to the Arts and Crafts Movement centred on the workshop of Ernest Gimson and the Barnsley brothers in the village of Sapperton, where this fine example of topiary is to be seen. The Arts and Crafts Movement drew its inspiration from the rural crafts of medieval times, and had considerable influence on garden design of the early 1900s.

Selborne, Hampshire

This cottage, with its topiary flanking the garden gate – a pawn and a bishop, perhaps? – is in the village made famous by the eighteenth-century naturalist Gilbert White, who recorded, in careful and vivid detail, the natural history of his village. Simple shapes such as these are ideal for the beginner in topiary; the more practised and ambitious topiarists progress to elaborate geometric shapes or represent- ations of almost anything that takes their fancy.

Kiddington, Oxfordshire

Broody hens, lightly rimed with frost, are touched with the same winter sunlight that warms the stone walls of this cottage in Kiddington, Oxfordshire. Without the distraction of the flowers that make cottage gardens so colourful in spring and summer, topiary can be enjoyed to the full in winter.

Kiddington, Oxfordshire

Still in Kiddington, these more elaborate, stylized birds are perched on a clipped hedge. As well as befitting the scale and character of a cottage garden, topiary as part of a low hedge is easier to manage than work on the grand scale that must be scaffolded for its annual clipping.

Minster Lovell, Oxfordshire

A handsome box spiral, framed by the arch over the entrance gate, dominates this front garden, even drawing the eye from the exuberant pink roses. In England, box usually needs clipping only once a year, after the last frosts of spring, though if the summer is as wet as legend would have it English summers always are, it may need another trim to tidy whiskery growths before autumn sets in.

Chipping Campden, Gloucestershire

Topiary need not be either representational or formally geometric. There is a wonderful congruity between the rounded lines of the thatched roof and the billowy, informal yet close-clipped hedge that seems to hold this Cotswold cottage in a comfortable embrace.

Kemerton, Hereford and Worcester

By its nature, topiary is full of fantasy. The yew arch in this garden, spanning the narrow path at the foot of the house wall, is transmogrified into a topiary bird surveying the garden. This is what might be achieved, with imagination and patience, by cutting into an existing ancient, free-growing yew planted by the cottage wall to fend off wind and harmful spirits. Yew does not mind being cut hard back into the old wood so long as it is well fed and watered after the operation.

Berriew, Powys

Unusually, these peacocks on their individual, tiered plinths, either side of the traditional straight, central garden path, have shaped but unclipped tails – which, supposing the unlikely proposition that realism has anything to do with topiary, is a more accurate representation of a real peacock's tail in full display than the neatly clipped version usually seen.

West Chiltington, Sussex

The simple shape of this golden topiary reminds one, more than anything, of an old-fashioned spice box – the kind with a circular centre compartment to hold a nutmeg grater under the raised portion and a series of divisions in the outer ring, where housewives used to keep not just their precious nutmegs, but also cloves for pomanders or apple pie, peppercorns for pickling, and cinnamon sticks for crushing onto sugared toast. This cottage garden has other traditional features, such as the fragrant honeysuckle on the porch and the wooden seat against the cottage wall, in the sun.

Lacock, Wiltshire

The unsophisticated topiary birds squatting on the boundary hedge, by drawing the eye to the foreground, give even greater depth to the expansive landscape beyond the garden, fading into a blue distance. Although Britain is a small island, and the south especially is densely populated, it is surprising just how many cottages still look out over such unspoiled rural views.

Great Tew, Oxfordshire

Great Tew is one of England's famously picturesque villages, and here, seeing it from across a field white with hoar frost, it is easy to understand why. These cottages are built on, and of, the limestone backbone of England, which in this region is rich ochre yellow in colour. The clipped hedges, comfortably rounded, barely qualify to be classed as topiary, perhaps, but they anchor the cottages to their setting.

East Lambrook, Somerset

If you are going to create your own topiary, using young trees, it is worth planning early what shapes you intend to make. You can start work on the base of your design even while waiting for the upper part to grow. Both the peacock and the spiral in this garden have a distinct plinth to stand on.

Alfriston, Sussex

This comfortable brick and thatch house in the cottage style has a yew by the chimney breast in the traditional manner, and a garden of clipped domes and a well-manicured hedge to contrast with the sharp spire of the village church right next door. On the kitchen-garden side of the hedge a clump of silvery cardoons adds yet another outline and colour to this composition of foliage and form.

Stoke Holy Cross, Norfolk

Box spirals, grown in tubs, are often seen flanking sophisticated town-house front doors, but they seem just as much at home by the door of this weatherboarded Norfolk cottage, half hidden by the leaning, untidy spires of foxgloves, white valerian and pink opium poppies that have seeded into the gravel.

Adorning the Cottage Wall

The fashion for adorning cottage walls and porches with climbers is not a recent one. Just as the poet John Clare urged cottagers to build a summer seat amid fragrant flowers, so – in the same 'little garden not too fine, enclosed with painted pales' – he liked to see 'woodbines round the cot to twine'. Another source of knowledge of English cottage gardens of that time is Miss Mitford, author of *Our Village*. Writing between 1824 and 1832, she described the cottage gardens of a Hampshire village, a composite in fact of several villages she knew well; the gardens of the country people in all their diversity, from the gentry and the farmers to the craftsmen and the labourers. In Miss Mitford's village, as in John Clare's imagination, the honeysuckle or woodbine was the most treasured of climbers, on account of its sweet fragrance, but grape-vines were almost as popular, with the great advantage of productivity: at least two dozen varieties hardy enough to grow outdoors in the south of England were known. One brick cottage had a clematis on one side and a rose on the other; on others grew jasmine, convolvulus, passion flower, and ivy. Her own cottage had walls 'old and weather-stained, covered with hollyhocks, roses, honeysuckles, and a great apricot tree'.

Owslebury, Hampshire

This cottage and garden would surely look quite familiar to Miss Mitford: the low wall, white-painted gate, path leading straight to a creeper-clad porch, and roses on the wall are as typical of the nineteenth century as of the late twentieth.

Owslebury, Hampshire

Through the white gate into the garden itself, for a closer look at the clematis and exuberant rose on the walls, and the carefree profusion of flowers, among them the blue love-in-a-mist (*Nigella damascena*) and violet-purple *Campanula glomerata* 'Superba', a selected form of the native British clustered bellflower.

Owslebury, Hampshire

The wild roses of England are modest in flower, if not in growth, but this more modern variety combines colour and profusion to look perfectly at home in a cottage garden. The diamond-paned window half-hidden behind an arching rose branch recalls the days when glass-making techniques were not advanced enough for large panes.

East Coker, Somerset

Honeysuckle is at its sweetest at night, when its fragrance carries far on the cool air. It has been allowed to grow freely, in traditional style, over the porch of this cottage. The native English *Lonicera periclymenum*, also known as woodbine, is as fragrant as any exotic honeysuckle, and some of its varieties, with names such as 'Early Dutch' and 'Late Dutch', are colourful as well, especially where the soft yellow blooms are touched with the sun to flush with maroon and purple.

Kemerton, Hereford and Worcester

When the cottage is built of honey-golden stone, it would be a shame to hide it beneath too profuse a growth of climbers. The gnarled ivy is just right in its restraint, leaving the upper storey bare to give full value to the shadows cast by the deep thatch overhang.

Kilmington, Wiltshire

Roses and honeysuckle wreath the mellow brick and flint walls, reaching to the eaves to insinuate their perfume through open bedroom windows in summer; more roses fill the borders in the garden. The roses known to the cottagers of old would be those that flower only once, but today there are many repeat-flowering varieties to choose from, to ensure a long season of flower.

Pitney, Somerset

The walls of this cottage are covered with clematis and roses, a classic combination to give a long season of flower. For a shorter season, but a greater impact, plant a summer-flowering clematis and a rose on the same wall, to flower at the same season. The classic summer-flowering clematis for cottage gardens is the indestructible violet-purple *Clematis × jackmanii* 'Superba'.

Pitney, Somerset

The rambler roses with blood of the wild musk rose in them almost all have small, white, deliciously fragrant flowers borne in large clusters in summer. England's own native musk rose, *Rosa arvensis*, grows wild in copses and hedgerows, and is as sweetly scented as any; it is the rose of Shakespeare's *A Midsummer Night's Dream*:

I know a bank where the wild thyme blows,
Where oxlips and the nodding violet grows,
Quite over-canopied with luscious woodbine,
With sweet musk-roses and with eglantine.

(Eglantine is John Clare's sweet brier, the wild *Rosa eglanteria* which was treasured for the fragrance of its leaves and flowers.)

The newer varieties, bred from musk roses introduced from southern Europe, were valued by Miss Jekyll in her cottage-inspired garden. What was new was the way in which she used the old cottage favourites with a painter's eye, to make beautiful pictures by deliberate design rather than happy accident. This tumble of musk roses over a grey stone wall, with only the green of foliage and the chartreuse froth of lady's mantle (*Alchemilla mollis*) as accompaniment, would surely have pleased her.

Alkerton, Oxford

Miss Jekyll greatly valued hostas, at a time when they had not the immense popularity they enjoy today. She grew them, as often as not, in large tubs which stood in a paved courtyard of her rather large cottage-style house. Here they have been set in a narrow bed among the stones, their bold leaves contrasting with the ferns growing in and at the foot of the wall and with the pleated fans and lime-green flowers of lady's mantle. The white-flowered creeper on the wall is a climbing hydrangea.

Rolvenden, Kent

The original intention for this pink *Clematis montana* might have been to cover the porch, but montanas are vigorous and untameable; it has reached the roof ridge and chimney of a Kent cottage, working its way under the tiles to emerge with a pink trail here and another there.

Swerford, Oxfordshire

A pink montana again, but here it is paired with mauve wisteria. Both introduced from the Far East in the early 1800s, they have made themselves completely at home in English cottage gardens. There is something far from exotic about the fragrance of wisteria; it recalls, more than anything else, the smell of a beanfield in flower, which would have been familiar to every cottager in the Middle Ages.

Hook Norton, Oxfordshire

Roses on the wall, foxgloves at their feet, a 'gothic' window, a wooden fence for a stone-built cottage: simple components, adding up to a picture that could be the result of happy accident or studied planning.

Owslebury, Hampshire

'Albertine', the rose around the window in this Hampshire garden, is a comparatively recent introduction – she dates from 1921. Although only once-flowering, and of lax growth with ferociously prickly stems, neither quite a climber nor properly a shrub rose, she was quickly adopted as a cottage garden favourite for the delicious, free-floating perfume from those coppery-pink blooms.

Lacock, Wiltshire

Even if there is nowhere to plant climbers at the foot of the cottage wall, with a little ingenuity there can be flowers around the windows. This window box spills over with marigolds, and pelargoniums – which almost everyone continues to call geraniums – tumble out of hanging baskets masking drainpipes or swinging from wall brackets.

Streatley, Berkshire

Almost every inch of wall-space on this cottage is covered with climbers, and for still more colour there is a hanging basket of candy pink geraniums near the door, and flowers growing in narrow borders along the base of the walls. The pink Japanese anemones are among the best of late summer and early autumn perennials, flowering with abandon in cottage gardens and grand domains alike.

A Medley of Flowers

Many of the flowers that we regard as belonging to cottage gardens were already considered old-fashioned in the early nineteenth century, as we learn in this poetic catalogue by John Clare:

> . . . the best flowers; not those of wood and fields,
> But such as every farmer's garden yields –
> Fine cabbage-roses, painted like her face,
> The shining pansy, trimm'd with golden lace,
> The tall-topped larkheels, feather'd thick with flowers,
> The woodbine, climbing o'er the door in bowers,
> The London tufts, of many a mottled hue,
> The pale pink pea, and monkshood darkly blue,
> The white and purple gilliflowers, that stay
> Ling'ring, in blossom, summer half away,
> The single blood-walls, of a luscious smell,
> Old-fashion'd flowers which housewives love so well,
> The columbines, stone-blue, or deep night-brown,
> Their honeycomb-like blossoms hanging down
> Each cottage-garden's fond adopted child,
> Though heaths still claim them, where they yet grow wild.

What John Clare does not tell us is how they were arranged. For this we must turn to Flora Thompson, who grew up in the neighbouring county of Oxfordshire:

Nearer the house was a portion given up entirely to flowers, not growing in beds or borders, but crammed together in an irregular square, where they bloomed in half-wild profusion. There were rose bushes there and lavender and rosemary and a bush apple-tree which bore the little red and yellow streaked apples in later summer, and Michaelmas daisies and red hot pokers and old-fashioned pompom dahlias in autumn and pinks and peonies already budding.

It seems clear that the aesthetic use of colour had little or no conscious place in these cottage gardens; for that we have to wait for Miss Jekyll and her painter's eye. But the artless jumbles of flower have their own charm, and such cottage medleys, direct inheritors of a long tradition, can be seen to this day around the cottages where so many generations of flowers have bloomed and gone.

Amberley, Gloucestershire

The spires of lupins and delphiniums and the silky blooms of scarlet oriental poppies, all jostling for space, are very much in the spirit of Flora Thompson's 'half-wild profusion'. Lupins can be grown as biennials, lined out in a spare plot to make their first season's growth, then discarded after flowering to make room for summer flowers. Interplant them with tulips to flower in spring among the lupins' fresh young foliage, and you ensure a long succession of colour from the same patch of ground.

Steeple Aston, Oxfordshire

The narrow strip of bright flowers on the outside of the garden fence would hardly have been possible in the days when geese, and perhaps even pigs, cows or sheep, were allowed to graze on the village common. The kaleidoscopic colours in this spring scene are contained within the straight lines that frequently character-ized cottage gardens, and which are to be seen in their grander imitations as well, formality of design combining with generous informality in the planting.

Ampney Crucis, Gloucestershire

Another spring picture, where primroses – both the lovely pale wildling and brightly-coloured forms – and daffodils, grape hyacinths and scarlet tulips crowd the beds around a small lawn where daisies grow. In both Gloucestershire and the neighbouring county of Oxfordshire the wild daffodil or Lent lily grows still in great numbers at the margins of meadows, and primroses stud grassy banks and hedgerows.

Stoke sub Hamdon, Somerset

Spring passes into summer, and yellow Welsh poppies and sky blue forget-me-nots bloom with pink bistort, meadow rue and pink columbines. John Clare was right to call columbines old-fashioned, for they were among the plants Thomas Tusser listed, and Gerard wrote that the flowers, sometimes blue, at other times red, purple or white, were 'things so famil-iarly known to all'.

Sherborne, Gloucestershire

Red valerian, orange California poppies, lupins, oriental poppies, golden feverfew and white shasta daisies, and the spires of pink and white foxgloves, form this summer medley. Though many people like the varied shades of foxgloves from white to deep, speckled rose-purple, it is easy to keep a white or apricot-pink strain pure by pulling out all the seedlings with a purple stain on the leaf stalk – they will have rose-pink or purple flowers, while those with wholly green leaf stalks will have white, apricot or cream flowers.

Evershott, Dorset

The brilliant scarlet flower in the left foreground is *Lychnis chalcedonica*, the Maltese cross or Jerusalem cross. It is of great antiquity in English gardens, dating from the time of the Crusades. It earned its name from the shape of its flowers, not because it was brought back from the Holy Land – its botanical name 'chalcedonica' suggests an origin in Asia Minor, in the Bosphorus region where stood the ancient town of Chalcedon.

Hatch Beauchamp, Somerset

Banks of brilliant blue delphiniums soar above the more lowly plants in this garden, framing the unspoilt rural landscape that forms the view from the cottage. The twin flower borders flanking the narrow path leading straight from gate to front door are typical of the cottage garden tradition.

Dolton, Devon

When none of the colours is harsh or strident, a kaleidoscopic mixture avoids jarring contrasts, especially in an emollient setting of whitewashed cottage and the green woods of the West Country. The tawny day lily against the cottage wall is an old plant, known in England by 1570 and grown by Gerard and, he tells us, 'in the gardens of Herbarists, and lovers of fine and rare plants'. He is scathing about the rapidity with which the flowers fade: 'the same day in the evening it shuts itself, and in a short time after becomes as rotten and stinking as if it had been trodden in a dunghill.' Clearly others were not put off by this exaggerated description, for it remains a favourite.

Itteringham, Norfolk

This two-up, two-down brick cottage with climbers on the walls and a bright jumble of flowers in the front garden is in a typical East Anglian village. The red opium poppies in the foreground are not native, but must have been introduced centuries ago, for in the Middle Ages, as still today, the seeds (which contain none of the drug) were scattered over bread dough to add flavour before baking. Thomas Tusser listed poppy as one of the herbs to be grown in the garden for physic; opium was used to relieve the pains of cholera, dysentery and childbirth.

Shottery, Warwickshire

In the garden of the cottage belonging to Anne Hathaway, Shakespeare's wife, at least some of the plants could have been familiar to the bard himself: the blue globe thistle (*Echinops ritro*) was an early arrival from Europe, known already in English gardens by 1570, and the dusty pink eupatorium is a British native.

Collingbourne Ducis, Wiltshire

Delphiniums and lupins, yellow loosestrife and lady's mantle, grow here with, for backdrop, a substantial black-and-white, thatched cottage. This is not the native yellow loosestrife, *Lysimachia vulgaris*, but its near relation introduced from Asia Minor in the nineteenth century, *L. punctata*, which has made itself so much at home as to have become a ditch weed in some parts of England. *Alchemilla mollis*, the lady's mantle of gardens, is also from Asia Minor, and there is, too, a British native lady's mantle of lesser beauty. Lady's mantle was thought to have magical properties because of the way the pleated, downy leaves catch pearls of dew – itself reputed to have great powers – in the night.

Ilmington, Warwickshire

Cottage garden plants old and new: hollyhocks in pastel shades, and a buddleja. *Buddleja davidii* is a fairly recent introduction (around 1890) which cottagers quickly took to their hearts, calling it butterfly bush because its fragrant spikes are visited by scores of butterflies sipping the honey-sweet nectar.

Dolton, Devon

This garden is in the newer cottage-garden tradition popularized, above all, by Margery Fish: close-packed plants leaving no bare soil for weeds to colonize, muted colours, an eye for foliage and for contrasts of outline. Margery Fish created a garden in Somerset which was to become the inspiration for a whole generation of gardeners; even those who never visited her garden were able, thanks to her books, articles and lectures, to feel that they knew it intimately.

Sherborne, Gloucestershire

The grey stone of this fine Cotswold cottage is enlivened by the cheery clashes of pink peonies, vermilion oriental poppies and mauve foxgloves, all amid the fresh green foliage of early summer. Children love to make poppies into dolls by turning back the petals to reveal the shaggy black stamens and velvety seed capsule, tying the petals into a 'dress' of scarlet silk with a blade of grass for the waist.

Brigsteer, Cumbria

Against the whitewashed walls of this long, low cottage, even under the grey, rain-washed skies of north-western England, reds and yellows are wonderfully vibrant. The teasel in the foreground, a native plant, was formerly used by clothiers to tease up the nap of newly-woven woollen cloth, the variety of choice being the fullers' teasel with recurved bracts rather than the ordinary wild teasel in which the bracts are straight and less effective at raising the nap. Despite its thistly looks, it is related not to the true thistles but to the blue-flowered scabious of England's chalklands.

Streatley, Berkshire

The warm red brick of this cottage tones with the assertive sunshine colours of a bed of dahlias and rudbeckias, with a scarlet rose, crimson hydrangeas and red-and-white fuchsias, all growing and flowering with abandon. The dusty blue shutters add a touch of cool colour.

Behind the Scenes
Outbuildings, Greenhouses and
Cottage Garden Produce

The great medieval staple, the broad bean, was mainly a field crop, but in their gardens, cottagers and yeoman farmers grew leeks, onions and garlic, curly kale, leaf beets and turnips, and perhaps peas for pease pottage, a thick mash of dried peas flavoured, for the more fortunate, with a ham bone. But even cottagers who depended on their gardens for subsistence grew not only vegetables, but also some herbs and flowers – above all those that could be used for home remedies, to add flavour to a necessarily simple diet, or in making country wines. Flowers grown for their own sake would have come a poor third in the competition for space in the little plots, where there might have to be room for a pig and a few chickens, and probably a beehive or two, as well as everything else. Bacon and the occasional fowl, plus the odd rabbit poached from the local lord of the manor, would be all the meat these cottagers on the margins of subsistence could expect.

For the more fortunate, productivity was not only to do with subsistence. Thus the ladies of Cranford, the village imagined by the nineteenth-century novelist Mrs Gaskell, spared no opportunity to

Hartland, Devon

An old apple tree spreads its canopy over a stone-tiled, ivy-clad outhouse beside a ditch. Striped clematis such as the one growing by the door generally hold their colour better in light shade, even in England where the summer sun is often veiled by a gentle, blue-grey haze.

perform small deeds of kindness such as saving rose petals for pot pourri, or lavender for strewing among the linen, for someone without a garden; and 'elegant economy' was practised by the ladies, who would have been mortified to admit that it was the economy of necessity.

Despite their own limited means, cottagers have for centuries grown plants that needed protection from the elements. Thomas Tusser's herbs and flowers for windows and pots, to be grown by the Elizabethan tenant farmer's wife, included amaranthus and French marigolds. By the mid-nineteenth century cottagers were growing pelargoniums and calceolarias and dahlias, and a whole range of annuals, some of which would have needed sowing under cover to be planted out after the frosts.

Sankyns Green, Hereford and Worcester

Before indoor sanitation, every cottage that was more than a hovel had its outdoor privy, sometimes a solidly-made little building, sometimes a movable earth closet. Today, if they survive, such outbuildings are likely to be used to keep garden tools and deckchairs, or to store onions, apples and dahlia tubers for the winter. The paved path to this brick and tile outbuilding means it can be reached dry-shod in all weathers. The fragrant honeysuckle over the door and roof, and the profuse planting around the little building, make it decorative as well as utilitarian.

Evershott, Dorset

Plastic sheeting and timber
make a simple but effective
greenhouse to raise seedlings
for summer bedding, including
the beautifully grown *Lavatera*
'Silver Cup' and *Malope trifida*
in the foreground. The mixture
of annual and perennial flowers
is typical of cottage gardens,
where floral apartheid has
never been the rule.

Market Bosworth, Leicestershire

There is a long tradition
among working men of
growing prize blooms and
vegetables, the bigger the
better, to be entered for the
village flower show. This
thatched cottage with its huge
pink cactus dahlias is in the
East Midlands, but the local
horticultural show is a country-
wide phenomenon. Like other
specialists' flowers –
chrysanthemums, gladiolus and
pelargonium among them –
dahlias are classified into
different groups, from the
shaggy cactus to the tightly
formal pompon, by way of
'waterlily', 'anemone-flowered',
'collarette' and 'decorative',
with further subdivisions for
size – giant, large, medium,
small and miniature.

Ilmington, Warwickshire

The small greenhouse no doubt contributes to the productivity of this vegetable patch, where scarcely an inch of bare soil is to be seen. It is skill in cultivation above all, though, that counts. However basic the cottagers' growing techniques may have been in earlier centuries – we simply have not the evidence from which to judge – it seems certain that by 1700 a good cottage garden would have provided its skilled owner with well-grown vegetables, herbs and fruit. Sowing under cover would enable the cottagers to produce earlier vegetable crops, to bridge the gap between the stored roots of winter and the first of the new season's greens. At first most of these early sowings would have been in pots or wooden seed trays set on indoor windowsills. The invention of plastic as a cheap substitute for glass has meant that in the late twentieth century a greenhouse of sorts, however basic, has come to be within the reach of those for whom the elaborate glasshouses of wealthy Victorians, or even a modern conservatory, would be an impossible dream.

Steeple Aston, Oxfordshire

Cottage gardeners have been environmentalists for generations, even if the word is new: they could ill afford to waste anything, and in the compost heap, household waste, weeds, clippings and the vegetable debris from the kitchen garden can all be recycled. There is no need of a purpose-built compost bin; a few planks serve well enough to keep the material together while it rots into a mound of rich, dark goodness. This compost, the manure and seepings from the pigsty, and night soil from the privy, were an invaluable source of nutrients for the soil. Old cottage gardens, long-cultivated, are often blessed with rich, dark soil thanks to the generations of gardeners who added every scrap of goodness to the soil for the sake of the crops it must yield.

Rampisham, Dorset

Even galvanized iron, cheap and utilitarian but never an object of aesthetic admiration, can have a certain charm when half masked by the bundles of sticks thrown over the roof and the row of beans that grows alongside. In front is a little rhubarb patch and the pots used to force the stems to tender pink succulence in early spring; further along the well-trodden path the scarlet runner-bean flowers yield to a medley of sweet peas.

Rampisham, Dorset

This little patch has something of everything – a bean row, sweet peas for picking, the old cottage garden plant *Lychnis coronaria*, familiarly known as dusty miller for its grey leaves, and a collection of the brightest annuals imaginable. Nothing is wasted, neither space – the path is as narrow as it can be – nor materials: the little shed in the background has been neatly patched up with old fertilizer sacks.

Sherborne, Gloucestershire

A cottage garden with vegetables and flowers side by side: delphiniums by the broad beans, and foxgloves near the potatoes. Foxgloves are natives of England, growing in woodland and copses, but they have long been grown in gardens, and once introduced, seed themselves so as to need no further care. Cottagers believed that potatoes and apples would last longer in store if foxgloves grew nearby, and cut flowers are slower to fade if foxgloves – or failing the flowers themselves, foxglove tea – are added to the vase. They contain digitalin, which acts upon the heart muscles to slow them down; foxglove tea may be good for cut flowers, but is highly dangerous as a beverage.

Brigsteer, Cumbria

This immaculately tended garden, with vegetables and flowers alongside each other, is in north-western England. The long, low cottage is typical of the northerly regions; in days gone by, one end of the building would be for the family and the other for their livestock.

Rampisham, Dorset

For many people, the sight of neat rows of vegetables, ready to harvest or promising a future crop, is as appealing as a flower garden. Few cottagers, however, resist the temptation to allow a few flowers into the vegetable garden, and this garden is no exception, with a clump of dusty miller (*Lychnis coronaria*) and a row of vivid annuals echoing the bright colours of scarlet runners and sweet peas in flower.

Charsfield, Suffolk

It may be no cheaper, these days, to grow your own vegetables than to buy them in the supermarket, and the choice is much wider in the shops; but there is nothing to beat the flavour of fresh-picked, home-grown produce, not to mention the pleasure of being, at least in part, self-sufficient as our forbears had no choice but to be. This cottage garden is neat and productive, and the scarecrow is more appropriate to the simple, even plain cottage than the strips of clattering glitter many people use today. Whether it is as effective against marauding birds is another matter.

Adderbury, Oxfordshire

The cottage gardens of nineteenth-century farm and estate workers would often have backed onto neatly fenced parkland, like this one. Feverfew has seeded itself here and there, and a row of scarlet runners seems entirely congruous amid the herbs and flowers. A clump of fennel is in full flower, promising a good crop of seed. In the Middle Ages fennel seeds were popular not only for their aniseed flavour; chewing the seeds in times of shortage helped to allay the pangs of hunger.

Dowlish Wake, Somerset

Even the smallest patch of ground can be made productive, if it is fenced or walled against marauding livestock, backed by a thick hedge to keep off the wind, and tended with care. The red valerian is allowed to bloom on the wall, but where the crops grow no weed remains to rob the soil of precious fertility.

Flintham, Nottinghamshire

The technique of growing apples and pears espalier-style is equally suitable for large gardens, where paths through the vegetable garden were often lined with espaliers, and small cottage gardens, where space is at a premium and an espalier or two could be tucked in between the vegetables and the flowers. In this garden an apple, cropping abundantly, is set among a typical cottage medley of annuals – cosmos and tobacco flower, dahlias and clary. The espaliered pear is garlanded with nasturtiums, of the old-fashioned variety with long, sprawling stems that are ready to climb into any nearby support. The seeds of nasturtiums can be pickled and used as a substitute for capers, while the edible flowers are decorative in a salad and the peppery-tasting leaves can be shredded with other salad leaves for extra flavour.

Apple 'Mini John'

Apples are among the most versatile of fruits for the cottage garden; between cookers and eaters, and the sharp crabs that make such delicious jelly, there is an apple for every use, and most of them keep well in store to provide fruit during the winter months and into the lean days of early spring before the new season's produce is ready. Many are highly decorative too, both in flower, and again in autumn when they ripen, though not many are quite as bright as this vivid red, free-fruiting variety.

Garden Seats, Bowers and Arches

The genuine labouring cottager might seldom have had time to sit in his garden; but when he did, he appreciated fragrant flowers about him, as we learn from the poet John Clare (1793-1864). Clare was not only a poet and melancholic but also a genuine cottager; the son of a poor labourer, he began his working life minding sheep and geese on the village common, and wrote of the rural life that was all he knew. When he tells us:

> Beside the threshold sods provide,
> And build a summer seat;
> Plant sweet brier bushes by its side,
> And flowers that blossom sweet

we can be sure he was painting a picture of the cottage gardens of his Northamptonshire village.

The tradition of embowering a garden seat in fragrant flowers was an old one. In *As You Like It*, William Shakespeare described 'the pleached bower, where honeysuckles, ripened by the sun, forbid the sun to enter' – perfect for the gentlewoman who wished, at the same time as playing at rusticity, to preserve her upper-class white-ness of complexion.

Ben Jonson, Shakespeare's slightly younger contemporary, was more ambitious. He wrote, in *Visions of Delight*, that

> . . . the blue bindweed doth itself enfold
> With honeysuckle and both these entwine
> Themselves with briony and jessamine,
> To cast a kind of odoriferous shade.

Daglingworth, Gloucestershire

This sturdy wooden seat is surrounded with a typical cottage medley of wild flowers and old-fashioned exotics: herb Robert, Welsh poppies in yellow and red cornfield poppies, mossy saxifrage, the southern European *Anthemis cupaniana*, with its vivid white daisies so like those of the moon daisies that flower later on English waysides, and silvery, aromatic cotton lavender (*Santolina*).

Sankyns Green, Hereford and Worcester

The contrast between neatly clipped hedges and the artless rusticity of the wooden seat in this garden is the very reverse of the simple but geometric lines of the seat nestling in wild flowers. The houseleeks (*Sempervivum*) growing in shallow clay pans either side of the seat are very like those often planted on tiled cottage roofs, where they thrive, apparently on air, lasting for years or even decades. To get them started, mix clay and some cow manure (from the fields, rather than full of straw from the byre) with water to make a paste, dab it on the roof where you want the houseleeks to grow, and after it has dried a little but is still tacky, pin the sempervivum rosettes in place. Christopher Lloyd, whose garden at Great Dixter in Sussex is in the grand cottage-garden manner, says a hairpin does nicely to hold the rosettes down until they have taken.

Crawley Down, Sussex

In the days before the invention of plastic patio furniture, pretty well the only alternative to wood for a garden seat was iron, painted to keep it from rusting. This white seat is embowered in roses for fragrance. Unlike Ben Jonson's odoriferous shade, the secluded corner is sunny and warm, dry underfoot thanks to the flagstones, and sheltered from the wind by the tile-hung house itself.

Alkerton, Oxfordshire

Sheltered in the angle between two walls, this sitting place with a seat and table is an ideal place to shell peas, read, write letters, eat summer meals, or simply enjoy the warmth of the sun, captured and reflected back by the ochre-yellow stone of the cottage walls.

Itteringham, Norfolk

The hammock and white lounger seat are set in the shade of an old apple tree; even in England's cool summers, dappled shade is welcome on bright, sunny days, and the modern cottage garden should be sufficiently labour-saving to allow for lazy moments in the hammock with a book or a cool drink at one's side.

Daglingworth, Gloucestershire

A mossy seat set in long grass, with the blue of evergreen alkanet at its feet and the tall umbels of Queen Anne's lace above, recalls one of the gardens that Flora Thompson wrote about in *Lark Rise to Candleford*: 'Between each section [of the garden] were thick groves of bushes with ferns and capers and Solomon's seal, so closed in that the long, rough grass there was always damp. Wasted ground, a good gardener might have said, but delightful in its cool, green shadiness.'

Solomon's Seal

Solomon's seal or David's harp, *Polygonatum multiflorum*, has been cultivated for hundreds of years. Gerard described its flowers resembling those of lily of the valley, followed by fruits 'of a black colour tending to blueness, and being ripe are of the bigness of Ivy berries, of a very sweet and pleasant taste.' The roots were also valued for their healing properties: 'The root of Solomon's seal stamped upon while it is fresh and green, and applied, taketh away in one night, or two at the most, any bruise, black or blue spots gotten by falls or women's wilfulness, in stumbling upon their hasty husbands' fists.'

Sankyns Green, Hereford and Worcester

Pergolas and arches in the gardens of mansions are apt to be imposing structures, but more simply constructed in cottage gardens they may serve the same functions: to mark a crossing path or the division between two sections of the garden, provide shade along a walkway, add a vertical note in a low planting or on a flat site, or simply provide a support for flowery, fragrant climbers. A pergola of roses, with hardy perennials sprawling over a path of bricks laid herringbone-fashion, makes a fragrant and shady passage from one part of the garden to another in this garden, belonging to a seventeenth-century yeoman farmer's house.

Crawley Down, Sussex

The rose-clad arch, casting a deep shadow on this sunny day, lures the visitor onward down the paved path between perennials and shrubs, many of them aromatic. The profuse planting, covering every inch of soil, is typical of cottage gardening.

Sankyns Green, Hereford and Worcester

Even the clipped dome of golden privet standing out so boldly against the purple beech hedge can hardly draw the eye from the idyllic rural scene, framed by a rose arch. Purists might argue that, in England, the cattle should be English, not a French Charolais cross – but their golden coats do tone beautifully with the honey-coloured roses.

Kilmington, Wiltshire

The coordinated colours of this planting around a rustic pergola of roses and clematis are typical of the more sophisticated style of cottage gardening. The soft shades of mauve and lilac, pink and purple and white, with silvery foliage in the background, not only blend harmoniously together; they also accord happily with the muted tones of the cottage walls and roof. The careful use of colour is wholly in the Picturesque tradition, which sought not merely the irregularity of the rustic, but also an aesthetic balance of light, mass and colour, to create a satisfying whole.

Owslebury, Hampshire

The term 'cabbage rose' is rather unflattering to describe the full-petalled, fragrant *Rosa centifolia*, though John Clare may have used it to refer to any fully double, old-fashioned rose. The pink and crimson roses in this garden, so gener-ous with bloom they have almost hidden the square wooden trellis that supports them, grow with blue campanulas and a single, perfectly placed white foxglove.

Water in the Cottage Garden

Even when drought conditions mean hosepipe bans in the garden, water continues to flow in the taps, at least for those of us living in the developed world. It is hard to imagine the chore of bringing water to the household that was the daily lot of most people until comparatively recently, but reminders exist in many a cottage garden – old wellheads and handpumps, once the only way to get water for drinking, cooking and washing, now do duty as a focal point amid plants or paving. And even now, in the remoter areas especially, the water for the household still comes from the well, even if it is now electrically pumped, effortlessly, to the taps. For drinking, well water is incomparably superior to the stuff the water companies supply.

Water had considerable commercial importance too; streams were channelled to create a forceful current strong enough to turn a waterwheel, which became the motive power to grind grain to flour between millstones. A number of these old mills are still in working order, and even when the grindstones are powered electrically, stone-ground, whole-grain flour is chosen by more and more people in preference to the denatured white substance of mass production.

Frampton-on-Severn, Gloucestershire

In days gone by every village would have its pond, where the villagers' ducks and geese could swim and their cattle and pigs come to drink. Nowadays, all too many of these ponds have either been filled in, or have dwindled to almost nothing as our growing water demands seriously lower the water table – some of the streams and rivers that fed the ponds of old have themselves dried to a trickle or entirely disappeared. In Frampton-on-Severn, however, the pond survives, and a family of swans are at home on its calm waters. their passage hardly ruffling the reflection of the fine village house standing across the road.

Lacock, Wiltshire

In this cottage garden the old well, seen from the garden gate, is now half-hidden among flowers. The stone surround appears to have been rebuilt, but the chain looks as though it has done generations of duty hauling buckets from the cool depths to the surface. The pampas grass that grows nearby (*right*) a native of the grasslands of South America, has long been a familiar inhabitant of English gardens, its fluffy plumes and arching blades contrasting with the rectangular outline of the wellhead.

130

Sankyns Green,
Hereford and Worcester

Pumping water by hand was
hard work, but the pump in
this cottage garden now stands
amid flowery containers and
borders that convey a sense of
repose rather than endeavour,
heightened by the use of soft
colours contrasting with the
strong, dark vertical of the
pump itself and the clean lines
of the stone wall and paving.

Lacock, Wiltshire

The vertical silhouette of an old handpump by a small pool is strikingly echoed by the slender steeple of a typically English parish church. The pink-flowered *Sedum spectabile* in the foreground is a typical cottage garden favourite, flowering in late summer and early autumn when it is popular with butterflies.

Hartland, Devon

The garden where these hostas, candelabra primulas and Siberian irises grow belongs to a working water-mill dating from 1249, near the north Devon coast. The owners have made good use of the millpond and leats (the open water-courses that guide the stream to the waterwheel) in creating a garden full of moisture-loving plants.

Hartland, Devon

In spring, after the wet winter characteristic of coastal western Britain, the leats are full and gushing with water. In a narrow bed between the watercourse and a retaining drystone wall, daffodils and coloured primroses grow beneath the branches of an old apple tree. Though these are modern varieties, the wild daffodil or Lent lily, and the pale wild primrose, might both have grown, untended, in the grass around the mill precincts when it was still in commercial use.

Hartland, Devon

In another spring scene in the same north Devon mill garden, the bright daisies of doronicums seem livelier than ever against the grey stone millhouse and the dark, water-soaked wood of the millwheel.

Huntonbridge, Buckinghamshire

The lawns and trees that surround this pool, captured in the soft light of spring, may seem rather too expansive to be called a cottage garden, yet like the garden in north Devon, this one too has been made around an old mill. In the absence of a stream constant and powerful enough to turn a waterwheel, windmills were used to grind corn, built tall and narrow so the sails could catch every breeze.

Kilmington, Wiltshire

Many of the plants that thrive near water have handsome foliage. Hostas, especially, have become popular in today's cottage gardens, where they seem just as much at home as in grander estates. The rounded, corrugated blue blades of *Hosta sieboldiana* contrast with a variegated hosta, the soft pleated fans of *Alchemilla mollis*, a bright candelabra primula and the spears of iris leaves. Only the variegated yellow flag, *Iris pseudacorus* 'Variegata', might have been familiar to a cottager of generations past; many of Britain's older garden plants are, like this, unusual forms of native plants.

Stoke sub Hamdon, Somerset

Even the smallest of pools can be the focus for a planting of moisture-loving and water plants. Here *Iris laevigata* and pink *Geranium endressii* grow beside dark water half-hidden by the flat pads of a water lily. These are introduced plants, but Britain has its own native water lilies: *Nuphar lutea*, commonly known as brandy bottle because of the bibulous smell of its yellow flowers, and *Nymphaea alba*, which counts among its common names the poetic 'lady of the lake' and 'swan among the flowers'.

**Blakemere,
Hereford and Worcester**

Here too, moisture-loving plants thrive beside a small pond, fitting easily, despite their exotic origins, into the gentle English landscape of woods, low hills and fields. The weeping willow's graceful outline is now so much part of the English scene that it might be thought a native tree; in fact it is Chinese, and was introduced only in about 1730, though it had already by then been long cultivated in mainland Europe.

Dolton, Devon

A simple wooden bridge crosses a ditch in which plants that like moisture grow lush and jungly to the exclusion of weeds – unless you count the ubiquitous foxgloves, and the frothy white cow parsley or Queen Anne's lace as weeds. These floral incidents pass against the more enduring backdrop of foliage: ferns, sedges, irises, and the rounded, lobed leaves of the umbrella plant (*Peltiphyllum peltatum*).

Cottage Garden Sophistication

Using the old cottage garden flowers mingled with more exotic introductions, Miss Jekyll and others developed the concept of the herbaceous border, or rather – as she called her own – the border of hardy flowers. She included shrubs, especially old cottage favourites with silvery foliage such as lavender and santolina or cotton lavender, and was not averse to using tender plants as well, especially in the red section of the border. Her great contribution was the artistic use of colour. At each end of the border was grey and glaucous foliage, accompanying at one end flowers of pure blue, white, palest yellow and pastel pink, and at the other, purple and lilac and mauve. From these soft tones the colours moved to deeper yellows, orange and finally fiery red at the centre of the border, ranging from the scarlet of oriental poppies, cannas and dahlias to the tall hollyhocks at the back, which her garden plan specifies as 'red and dark'. She also made gardens of a single colour or a narrow harmony, gold, orange, grey or blue, which have inspired countless plantings since and which are easier to emulate in a small garden than full-spectrum borders.

Hidcote Bartrim, Gloucestershire

The revival of hedges and walled enclosures, during the Edwardian era when Miss Jekyll was at the height of her powers, owes a great deal to the little enclosed gardens of England's cottages. One of the finest of England's large gardens in which hedges divide the garden into intimate 'rooms' is Hidcote, in Gloucestershire, created by Major Lawrence Johnston in 1905. Vita Sackville-West, who knew it well, certainly saw it as a cottage garden 'on the most glorified scale'. The gardens of the village of Hidcote Bartrim have their own smaller scale charm too; here a thatched cottage is rimmed by the chartreuse froth of lady's mantle, and the pale-flowered *Fuchsia magellanica molinae* is flanked by the golden form of *Lonicera nitida*, all harmonizing with the warm-toned Cotswold stone.

Alfriston, Sussex

Miss Jekyll thought highly of sweet Cicely (*Myrrhis odorata*), with its handsome ferny foliage early in the year and graceful white flower heads like Queen Anne's lace. Thomas Tusser lists it as one of the herbs to be grown for physic; it also has the great merit of adding sweetness to stewed fruit without the need for sugar. In the days when cottagers depended on the honey from their row of hives for all the needs we would now meet by buying a bag of sugar, this was a valued attribute. Here sweet Cicely grows with the green-flowered Corsican hellebore beside a Sussex house of the style known as Wealden, characterized by the little jutting upper floor at either end of the building, beneath the steeply pitched thatched roof. Wealden houses were built for well-to-do yeoman farmers, principally in the region known as the Weald of Kent and Sussex, from the fourteenth to the early sixteenth century.

Sibford Ferris, Oxfordshire

The components of this spring planting are of the simplest – Spanish bluebells in white, pink and blue, and plum-pink columbines, with touches of grey foliage – yet they create a satisfying harmony that wakes up the border in preparation for summer.

Blakemere,
Hereford and Worcester

Two views of a garden near Leominster, in Herefordshire, where colour is used with great subtlety to harmonize with the muted tones of the half-timbered cottage with its square-panelled framing. In one, the haze of flower of an ornamental grass is echoed by the tawny day lily and set off by the gentle lilac blue of the bell-flower *Campanula lactiflora*. In the other, the muted pink of the masterwort, *Astrantia maxima*, is separated from the yellow, black-stemmed spires of *Ligularia* 'The Rocket' by the rounded, glaucous-blue leaves of a hosta and the slate-blue helmets of monkshood.

Sankyns Green, Hereford and Worcester

Half-timbering again, this time with brick, is the setting for a wall-backed border in a Worcestershire garden. The choice of bearded irises in soft sienna brown and old-gold is inspired. To the left, the rich purple of the perennial wallflower known as 'Bowles's Mauve' is backed by the golden-variegated form of an old cottage garden favourite, the climbing summer jasmine. In the centre are white columbines.

Elsewhere in the same garden (*right*), the colour theme changes to pink and mauve and white, with silver and grey foliage, in a group of low, hummocky plants in a two-level raised bed. Much of the colour comes from pinks, which thrive in the free drainage of the higher level.

Pitney, Somerset

In the nineteenth century many of the roses we now describe as old-fashioned were first introduced. Here grow two varieties of *gallica* rose, 'Tuscany Superb' and 'Charles de Mills', flanking campanula-bordered stone steps leading to a sundial. The garden has been made around a group of seventeenth-century stone farm buildings, and stone has been used to good effect to give form to the billowy outlines of the roses which fill the garden.

(*Right*) *Geranium psilostemon* flaunts its magenta, black-eyed flowers in front of a stone bird bath. Hardy geraniums are ideal companions for old roses, of which there are many in this garden; their colour ranges are complementary, and many of the geraniums have attractive, weed-excluding foliage as well. Some are natives of Britain, including the blue meadow cranesbill, which has given rise to double-flowered forms in blue, purple and white, perfect for the cottage garden as, unlike the singles, they do not seed themselves around.

Sankyns Green, Hereford and Worcester

Like double flowers, variegations often occur spontaneously and would have been treasured by farmers' wives with an eye for the curious and unusual. The variegated comfrey growing in this Worcestershire garden is an ornamental form of a plant that has many uses, though for utility one would choose the plain green form. A comfrey poultice eases bruises, ulcers and strains, and was even said to be effective for broken limbs – potent magic indeed, when a

broken bone could mean amputation, and certain loss of the ability to support one's family. Comfrey leaves make a nourishing compost said to increase the yield of crops, and they can even be cooked into something rather like spinach. Its virtues have been long known; it is one of the plants listed by Jon the Gardener in *The Feaste of Gardening*. The use of its handsome variegated form in this carefully thought-out planting shows how far the cottage garden has evolved from medieval times when cottagers relied on their little plots for their very survival.

Author's Acknowledgements

Andrew Lawson has been a delight to work with on what I hope will be the first of many collaborations. As ever, Michael Dover has been the ideal editor, always encouraging and supportive, ably backed by Emma Way and Richard Atkinson. And grateful thanks go to the owners of all the cottage gardens, in all their diversity, that feature in this book. Without them, and all the others we could not include, England's gardening heritage would be diminished. Grand gardens are fine to visit; but cottage gardens are for living with.

Photographer's Notes

For a self-taught photographer like myself, the earlier books in this series have been an inspiration. The first one, Candida Lycett Green's *English Cottages*, with photographs by the late Tony Evans, set the highest standards possible. Note that in Tony Evans's pictures there is hardly a TV aerial or an electric power line in sight. Early on in this project I rejected gardens that suffered from a glut of wires, but I was soon forced to revise this criterion. It is as if the power companies have converged on all the prettiest cottage gardens and strung them with cables. Or it could be that the best gardens are created in an attempt to deflect the gardener's eyes from all the wirework.

Again, from earlier volumes I have picked up advice by photographers I admire, like Clive Boursnell and George Wright. It is no coincidence if my technical tips match theirs. My equipment was 'state-of-the-art' when I bought it, but it is now hopelessly outmoded. I swear by my Canon F1, which the makers have now made redundant in favour of flashier electronic models. Again, my light meter is an old war-horse, a Weston Euromaster, and I adjust exposures manually. My favourite film is Kodachrome 25, which I sometimes warm up a bit with an 81A filter. This is the perfect film on those rare English days when the air is still and the light bright but diffused with thin cloud. On the more common days of grey murk, I resort to Fuji Velvia, which miraculously seems to bring light into the gloom. It is best unfiltered. Graduated filters, though, are helpful to bring the sky down to the same tonal scale as the land.

As for lenses, I tend to use the longest lens that the subject will allow. 85mm is my favourite, as it tends to bring the elements of the composition closer together, without too much distortion of space that the longer telephotos impose.

However in many of these pictures I have tried to include the complete garden and wide-angled lenses were unavoidable. I used a 35mm, 28mm, 24mm sometimes and on one occasion a 20mm when I could not stand any further back. I regret that all these lenses make small spaces seem larger. Whenever buildings appear, the Canon 35mm shift lens is invaluable. The important thing is to use a spirit level to ensure that the camera is horizontal, and then, as if by magic, you can rack up the lens so that the sides of a building remain vertical. It goes without saying that I always use a tripod.

Every landscape and garden photographer will tell you that the most important factor in a picture is being there at the right time. For me that is dawn, when the sunlight is soft, and filtered by a light mist. Then it becomes a logistical problem to be at the maximum number of gardens in the finite time available. My advance research was condensed into a road map of England with each promising cottage represented by a red dot. My ambition was far greater than my achievement, and there remain so many dots uncovered that I could do another complete book. I am sorry for all the wonderful cottage gardens that I never reached.

I am most grateful to Judy Dod for coordinating the research and to all the kind people who recommended gardens in their areas. Special thanks to Patrick Taylor and to Ethne Clarke, and also to Mrs Graeme Anton, Mrs Nigel Azis, Angela Baker, Sandra Burbidge, Gill Curtis, Jennifer Faber, Mervyn Feesey, Elizabeth Fleming, Daphne Foulsham, Arthur Gooch, Daphne Heald, Marion Henderson, Gillian Hill, Carolyn Lindsay, Bridget Marshall, Lavinia Mowbray, Nicholas Payne, Roger Pringle, Sarah Stafford, Mrs Robert Stone, Mariel Toynbee, Yvonne Toynbee, Witold and Heather Wondrausch. Above all I am indebted to the garden owners who, in these insecure times, were trusting enough to allow a perfect stranger to appear out of the blue and tramp around their gardens with his camera.

Bibliography

Fish, Margery: *Cottage Garden Flowers* (Collingridge, 1961)

Genders, Roy: *The Cottage Garden and the Old-Fashioned Flowers* (Pelham Books, 2nd edition, 1983)

Lloyd, Christopher: *The Cottage Garden* (Dorling Kindersley, 1990)

Scott-James, Anne: *The Cottage Garden* (Allen Lane, 1981)

Whiten, Faith & Geoff: *Making a Cottage Garden* (Bell & Hyman, 1985)

Index

Bold type indicates a reference in the main text. All other references are to captions.